Mysterious Encounters

Witches

by Rachel Lynette

KIDHAVEN PRESS

An imprint of Thomson Gale, a part of The Thomson Corporation

THOMSON
™
GALE

Detroit • New York • San Francisco • New Haven, Conn. • Waterville, Maine • London

THOMSON
GALE ™

© 2007 Thomson Gale, a part of The Thomson Corporation.

Thomson and Star Logo are trademarks and Gale and KidHaven Press are registered trademarks used herein under license.

For more information, contact

KidHaven Press

27500 Drake Rd.

Farmington Hills, MI 48331-3535

Or you can visit our Internet site at http://www.gale.com

LIBRARY OF CONGRESS CATALOGING-IN-PUBLICATION DATA

Lynette, Rachel.
 Witches / by Rachel Lynette.
   p. cm.—(Mysterious encounters)
 Includes bibliographical references and index.
 ISBN-13: 978-0-7377-3643-4 (hardcover)
 1. Witches—Juvenile literature. 2. Witchcraft—Juvenile literature. I.
 Title.
 BF1566.L96 2007
 133.4'3—dc22
                                                           2007006976

ISBN-10: 0-7377-3643-7

Printed in the United States of America

Contents

Chapter 1

Witches Yesterday and Today

Many people think of a witch as an ugly old woman who dresses in black robes and wears a pointed hat. She also has a black cat, flies around at night on a broomstick, and knows how to mix potions and perform a variety of evil spells. This

Myths and fairy tales about witches—including the story of Hansel and Gretel, pictured here—have fueled peoples' imaginations for centuries.

The famous 1939 movie *The Wizard of Oz* features a good witch, Glinda, pictured, as well as the Wicked Witch of the West.

is the image of a witch that has been passed down in countless folk and fairy tales.

Greek myths contain several witchlike characters. Perhaps the most well known of these is Hecate, the goddess of **sorcery**, who was thought to rule the spirit world. Another witchlike character is the monstrous Medusa, who had snakes for hair and could turn people to stone just by looking at them.

People's ideas about what witches were like evolved further in the early 1600s when Shakespeare wrote about three witches in the play *Macbeth*. In the 1800s the Brothers Grimm authored many stories, including *Snow White* and *Hansel and Gretel*, that feature frightening witches. Today, witches continue to fascinate both children and adults. In modern stories, witches are not always wicked and ugly. *The Wizard of Oz* features two witches, one who is wicked and one who is good. In the *Harry Potter* series, witches can also be both good and evil.

But witches are not just found in stories. Many people say that they have encountered witches in real life. Some people even claim to be witches themselves.

What Is a Witch?

A witch is a person, usually a woman, who uses magic to help or to hurt other people. A witch's magic might include casting spells, mixing potions, creating charms, communicating with the dead, and predicting the future.

In ancient times people who claimed to be witches were often honored and respected members of the community. Although they may not have actually performed supernatural acts, they did know a great deal about healing, plants, and the natural world. These ancient witches used their knowledge to heal sick people and help with childbirth. Because they were thought to be wise, people came to them for advice in matters of child rearing, love, money, and even the planting of crops. However, as Christianity spread throughout Europe in the Middle Ages (500–1500), people began to fear and **persecute** witches.

Most Christians in the Middle Ages believed that witches got their supernatural powers from the devil. They believed that witches were evil and that by using

Most Christians in the Middle Ages believed that witches got their supernatural powers from the devil, thereby branding witches as evil.

magic they were breaking God's commandments. The Bible states several times that witches and witchcraft are not to be tolerated. In the book of Exodus, God commands believers to kill women who perform magic, saying, "Do not allow a sorceress to live."[1] Many Christians took these words literally. Historians have estimated that more than 300,000 accused witches were killed throughout Europe in the Middle Ages.

Witches in the Middle Ages

Life was very difficult during the Middle Ages. Most people were poor and spent their lives working hard just to feed themselves and their families. People, often children, frequently died of horrible diseases like tuberculosis, small pox, and bubonic plague. Babies and mothers frequently died in childbirth. In addition, women in the Middle Ages were often treated more as property than as people. They rarely held positions of power and were expected to be quiet and obedient to their fathers and husbands.

People were also very **superstitious** during this time. They did not understand things about the world that science later explained. Most people believed that events like unexpected snow storms or illness were caused by supernatural powers. When something bad happened, people often blamed a

During the Middle Ages, events that could not be readily explained, such as an illness or a sudden weather change, were often blamed on women in the community who were accused of using witchcraft.

False Confessions

People accused of witchcraft were often brutally tortured until they confessed to being witches. In countries where torture was not allowed, they were told that if they confessed they would not be executed. Many people made up their confessions in order to avoid pain or death.

woman in the community. They would accuse her of using witchcraft to cause the unfortunate event. Often these women were old, unmarried, and poor. Women who did not attend church or who were not well liked by the community were also likely to be accused as witches. Such women were easy targets. They could not protect themselves, and usually no one cared enough about these women to help them once they were accused.

People frequently reported incidences of witchcraft to the authorities. In most cases the suspected witch would then be arrested and often tortured until she confessed. Most accused witches were put to death. Witches were executed in many gruesome and horrible ways, but usually a witch was hanged or burned alive.

Who Encountered Witches?

In the Middle Ages it was not uncommon for anyone to have an encounter with a witch, even a child. Children who encountered witches often appeared to be suffering from terrible fits. They would moan and scream, hurt themselves and others, and appear to be in horrible pain. These children claimed they had been bewitched by someone in the community. Often this was a person who had been unkind to them in the past.

Women also frequently claimed to encounter witches. Often the witch was a person in the community with whom they did not get along. This was es-

Although many people claimed to have encountered witches during the Middle Ages, it was more common for women and children to encounter witches than men.

Wicca and the Devil

Many people believe that Wiccans worship the devil, but this is not true. Wiccans may worship a variety of gods and goddesses, but they do not worship Satan.

pecially common if something bad happened soon after a quarrel. For example, if a woman's milking cow died suddenly or her child got sick, she might claim out of revenge that another woman in the community had used witchcraft to cause the misfortune.

Although men did not seem to encounter witches as much as women, they played a major part in persecuting the accused witches. Male preachers often spoke against witchcraft in their sermons. Men also tortured accused witches in order to get them to confess. In addition, men acted as judges, juries, and examiners in witch trials and as executioners when witches were sentenced to death.

Witches Today

Today, people rarely believe that they are the victims of witchcraft; however, there are thousands of people who claim to actually be witches. These people are part of a growing religion called Wicca. Wicca is based on the ancient **pagan** religions that many people followed before Christianity. Wiccans often meet in groups called

Followers of the Wiccan religion often wear this symbol, called a pentagram. It represents the earth, air, fire, water and the spirit.

covens where they practice witchcraft and cast a wide variety of spells. There are spells to bring good things like love and success. There are spells of healing and spells of protection. According to Zsuzsanna Budapest, a leader in Wiccan spirituality, these spells can influence the physical world to some extent:

> The Wicca craft is not based on faith but on observation. It is a way to bend nature this way and that: to make rain, stop storms, heal wounds . . . in other words to aid and protect life.

> The built-in safety latch, however, is Nature's wisdom. What must happen will, no matter how many spells you cast; what won't happen won't. Within the possibilities we can petition and communicate, and things do come true. But Nature will not "obey" humans.[2]

Although witches are not often persecuted today, modern witches are keenly aware that many women were killed because they were thought to be witches. Wiccans often honor these women in their **rituals**.

Chapter 2

The Witches' Wrath

Most people who lived in Europe in the Middle Ages tried to live their lives as good Christians. They attended church regularly, where they frequently heard frightening sermons about the evil practice of witchcraft. They believed that a witch could curse someone simply by looking at them. People began to fear that their own neighbors might be witches. Healers were especially feared. It was thought that if healers could use supernatural powers to cure the sick, they could also use them for evil purposes.

Seeking Revenge

In 1581 Grace Thurlowe accused a woman of being a witch, although the woman had once cured

During the Middle Ages, those found guilty of being a witch were often put to death by hanging.

Thurlowe's son. Thurlowe lived in the small town of St. Osyth, England. When her young son Davy fell ill, she asked Ursula Kempe to look at the child. Kempe was a **midwife** who was also known for "unwitching" the sick. This meant that she could remove curses and spells. Kempe sat by the sick child and while holding his hand repeated three times the **incantation**, "A good childe, howe, art thou laden."[3] The child quickly recovered, and Thurlowe was sure that Kempe had cured him.

A few months later Thurlowe gave birth to a healthy baby girl, and Kempe offered to care for the new baby. Even though Kempe had cured her son, Thurlowe was still frightened by her witchcraft and refused her offer. Kempe was offended but made no threats. Soon after, the baby girl fell out of her cradle, broke her neck, and died.

Thurlowe did not accuse Kempe of killing her baby at this time. Instead, she hired Kempe to cure her **rheumatism**. Kempe agreed, and although Thurlowe was cured almost immediately, she refused to pay Kempe the agreed-upon fee. Kempe went away muttering that she would have her revenge. A few days later Thurlowe's rheumatism returned worse than before.

It was only after her rheumatism returned that Thurlowe became convinced that Kempe had not only betwitched her but was also responsible for her baby's death. She told the authorities, and Kempe was accused of being a witch. She was put

Outspoken Women

Women in the Middle Ages were considered to be inferior to men. They were rarely educated and instead taught to be quiet and obedient to their husbands. Outspoken women were thought to be ungodly and were often accused of being witches.

on trial, found guilty, and hanged for practicing witchcraft.

Witches in the Family: The Pendle Witches

Women who were healers often passed that skill to their children, especially the girls. This may be why many people believed that witchcraft ran in families. Sometimes an entire family was suspected of being witches. The Devices were a poor family who lived in the Pendle Forest near Lancaster, England. In March 1612 Alizon Device met John Law, a peddler, on the road. She asked him to sell her some pins, but the peddler refused because he did not want to break open a whole packet of pins just to sell her a few. Device cursed the peddler and he immediately had what was probably a stroke. The peddler survived, but was lame on one side.

Someone to Blame

The old women who acted as the village healers did the best they could to cure the horrible diseases that were common in the Middle Ages. But they often failed. When someone died, the healer was often blamed and accused of being a witch.

This grave claims to mark the burial site of one of the witches tried in the famous Pendle witches trials of 1612.

Device confessed to paralyzing John Law, claiming that she did so with the help of a large black dog to whom she had given her soul. According to Alizon's confession, "there appeared unto her a thing like unto a blacke dogge: speaking unto her . . . and desiring her to give him her soule, and he would give her power to do any thing she would."[4] Alizon may have confessed because she did not understand how serious a crime witchcraft was and thought that she would be pardoned.

Alizon Device also accused other members of her family as well as another family of being witches and selling their souls to spirits in the form of animals. Family members testified against other family members, blaming each other for deaths and other misfortunes that had occurred in the community.

In the end ten accused witches were hanged for causing the deaths of seventeen people. Alizon Device as well as her mother and brother were among those executed.

Witches and Familiars

Animals, like Alizon Device's black dog, are often involved in witch encounters. Witches are known for keeping **familiars**, magical animals that do their bidding. In the mid-1500s three women in Chelmsford, England, were accused of using a white cat called Satan to harm other people.

Satan first belonged to Elizabeth Francis, who was accused of using the cat to kill a man who had refused to marry her. She was also accused of using

Witches are known for keeping familiars, magical animals that help carry out their owners' witchcraft.

This illustration depicts witches in the form of their animal familiars showing loyalty to the devil.

Satan to kill her own baby and later to lame her husband. Francis would give orders to the cat, who she claimed would answer her in English. Francis rewarded the cat with drops of her own blood.

Years later Francis traded the cat to her neighbor Agnes Waterhouse for some cakes. Waterhouse claimed that the cat did whatever it was told to do and received drops of Waterhouse's blood as a reward. Waterhouse confessed that over the years, she used the cat to kill several animals and people, including her own husband.

Waterhouse's eighteen-year-old daughter Joan was accused of using Satan to get revenge on Agnes Brown, a young neighbor who refused to give Joan bread and cheese. Twelve-year-old Agnes testified that Satan came to her several times in the form of a black dog with horns and the face of an ape. According to Agnes, "he came with a knife in his mouth and asked me if I were not dead and I said no I thanked god, and then he said if I would not die that he would thrust his knife to my heart but he would make me to die."[5] The creature did not kill Agnes, but it frightened her so badly that she became lame in her left leg.

The three women were tried in 1566 for practicing witchcraft. Joan Waterhouse was found not guilty. Agnes Waterhouse was found guilty and hanged. Francis escaped death this time. She was found guilty at another trial several years later and hanged.

The Bell Witch

Most witch encounters have involved people who are still alive, but John Bell and his family were tormented by a witch who claimed to be the spirit of someone who had died. Bell lived in Red River, Tennessee, where he had been involved in a dispute over land with his neighbor, Kate Batts. Batts swore on her deathbed that she would seek revenge on Bell.

In 1817 the Bell family began hearing strange noises in their house. They heard a woman crying, singing, and quoting the Bible. During the night the children often had their blankets thrown off of them by an invisible force. The witch especially targeted Bell's youngest daughter, Betsy, pulling her hair and slapping her. The witch was also responsible for Betsy's broken engagement to a neighbor, Joshua Gardner. Whenever the two were alone together, the witch would torment them until Betsy broke up with the man in 1821.

The witch especially hated John Bell, whom she vowed to kill and apparently did on December 20, 1820. Bell's health was declining when he died, but it appeared that it was not the illness that killed him. The family found a small bottle of poison near his body, which the witch claimed to have given him. At his funeral, she laughed and sang loudly.

Although the Bells kept the witch a secret at first, they eventually told their neighbors and soon the witch was known throughout the community. Hundreds of people claimed to have encountered

Carney Bell, pictured, is the great-great-great-great-grandson of John Bell. The Bell family claimed to have been tormented by the spirit of a dead witch from 1817 to 1821.

her, including General Andrew Jackson who would later become president of the United States. The Bell witch disappeared in 1821, but people claim that the land the Bells lived on is still haunted.

Over the years many people have claimed to have encountered witches. Many also claim that they were the victims of witchcraft. But in many cases history has shown that the real victims were the witches themselves, many of whom were falsely accused and executed for crimes they did not commit.

Chapter 3

Witch Hunts

itch hunts were common from 1450 to 1700 in the central regions of Europe. Witch hunts usually started with a few women or even just one woman being accused of practicing witchcraft. When brought to trial, the accused were often lied to and told that their lives would be spared if they named other members of the community who practiced witchcraft. People accused their neighbors, their friends, and even their family members. Those who were accused were arrested and many of them accused still more people. No one was safe. In some villages almost no women were left when the witch hunts were over.

Many people who were accused of witchcraft turned around and accused others, often falsely, in the hope of sparing their own lives.

Victim of Torture

More witches were killed in Germany than in any other country. The hunts were not just limited to women. Many children were also accused. Even men in positions of power were not safe. In 1628 Johann Junius, the mayor of Bamburg, Germany, was arrested for witchcraft. Under torture, several of his neighbors had reported that he had been present at witches' gatherings and had been seen talking with the devil.

Junius did not confess right away. He did his best to withstand the torture, but when the executioner told him that he would be tortured until he confessed, Junius gave a false confession. He was then told that his confession would not be accepted by the court unless he named other witches. Again he refused, but the torture proved too much to bear. When shown a list of names, he agreed that those people had been at the gathering.

Shortly before he was burned at the stake, Junius managed to write a letter to his daughter that was smuggled out of the prison by a guard. In it he proclaims his innocence and tells her of the torture:

> And then came—God in highest Heaven have mercy!—the executioner, and put the **thumbscrews** on me, both hands bound together, so that the blood ran out at the nails and everywhere, so that for four weeks I could not use

A particularly cruel death for those found guilty of being a witch was being burned at the stake, as depicted in this German newsletter from 1555.

my hands, as you can see from the writing. . . . Thereafter they first stripped me, bound my hands behind me, and drew me up in the **strappado**. Then I thought heaven and earth were at an end; eight times did they draw me up and let me fall again, so that I suffered terrible agony.[6]

Torments of a Child

Many witch hunts were fueled by the accusations of children. The testimony of children, some as young as two years old, was allowed in court. Confused and frightened children were frequently tricked into testifying against their own parents. Other children seemed to fall into fits and accused adults in their community of bewitching them.

In 1696, after Scotland had already seen quite a bit of witch hunting, eleven-year-old Christian Shaw

Swimming a Witch

One way to see if someone was a witch was to bind her hands and feet and throw her into deep water. If the person floated, it meant that the water had rejected her and she was a witch. If she sank, she was innocent—but also probably drowned.

In Europe untold numbers of innocent people were put to death during the height of the witch hunt era from 1450 to 1700.

began having horrible fits. During her fits, which lasted for days at a time, she would thrash and scream, claiming that she was being stabbed with knives. She accused two women—the family's maid Katherine Campbell and an old widow named Agnes Naismith who frequently begged at the household—of sending their spirits to cut her open. No one wanted to believe such a thing, and at first the two women were not arrested.

The family took Christian to the city of Glasgow to see an expert. On the trip she began to cough up little bundles of hair, bones, pins, stones, twigs, feathers, and other small objects. The bundles were dry and did not appear to come from her stomach.

Tricks of the Trade

To prove someone was a witch, a court-appointed pricker would prick her skin with a special needle. If the person felt no pain and did not bleed, she must be a witch. But many prickers had special trick needles that retracted into the handle.

The expert in Glasgow was baffled. The family returned home and the fits got worse. Christian told her family that she was being tormented because during the summer she had been taken to a witch's circle where the devil promised her many wonderful things if she would become a witch and kill her little sister. She had refused.

Christian continued to have violent fits and to accuse more people in the community of being witches. Finally, people started to believe. Twenty-one people were arrested and tried, and seven were found guilty and hanged as witches. The accused witches included two brothers ages eleven and fourteen and a woman named Margaret Lang who was known for her goodness and faith. Christian went on to live a normal life and never expressed regret about causing the death of seven people.

The Salem Witch Hunts

Witch hunts were not limited to Europe. They also happened in the New World. The most famous American witch hunt took place in 1692 in Salem, Massachusetts. Salem was a **Puritan** township of about 500 people.

The hunts began with nine-year-old Betty Parris, the daughter of the town's reverend, and her eleven-year-old cousin Abigail Williams. The two girls were often watched by the Parris's servant Tituba. Tituba was from Barbados and told the girls incredible stories of magic and played games with them to predict the future. After one of these games, Betty started to have horrible fits during which she shrieked and moaned, thrashed about violently, and threw things. Soon Abigail began having

Tituba, right, spins tales of magic to her young charges Betty Parris and Abigail Williams.

fits too, and it was not long before other young girls in the village also started acting strangely.

The girls claimed they were being tormented by the spirits of witches. At first they would not say who these witches were, but when pressured by the adults in the community they began to name their tormentors. The first three women to be named were the servant Tituba, a beggar named Sarah Good, and a sickly old woman named Sarah Osburne.

The girls testified in court against the women they accused, often having dramatic fits while being questioned. Ann Putnam, one of the most active accusers, gave this testimony against Sarah Osburne: "I saw the Apperishtion of sarah osborn the wife of Allexandar osborn who did immediatly tortor me most greviously by pinching and pricking me dreadfully and so she continewed most dreadfully to afflect me."[7]

The girls continued to accuse people, mostly women, of witchcraft. Whenever a person was named, she was immediately arrested and hauled off to prison to await trial. Although many of the women named were old, poor, or disliked by the community, at least one woman, Rebecca Nurse, was well regarded and known for her religious devotion and good works. Many came forward to proclaim her innocence, but in the end the fits of the girls won out and she was hanged. No one was safe from the girls' accusations.

One girl throws a fit, bottom right, while a woman provides dramatic testimony during one of the Salem witch trials.

One of the afflicted girls, a servant named Mary Warren, at one point admitted to lying about the fits and claimed that the other girls were also lying. The other girls immediately accused her of being a witch and she was arrested. When she stood trial, she changed her story and said that the girls were telling the truth after all. She was released and went back to having fits and making accusations with the other girls.

Seeking Attention

Most people do not believe that the girls in Salem were really being afflicted by witches. Many people believe that the girls pretended to be tormented because they enjoyed being the center of attention in a time when children, especially girls, were expected to be obedient and quiet.

By the fall of 1692 eighteen men and women had been hanged for practicing witchcraft, four had died in prison, and one man was crushed to death by rocks when he refused to stand trial. Over a hundred more awaited trial in jails around the county. The girls' stories were finally being doubted, as many of the accused had good reputations and were of high standing in the community. On October 8 the governor outlawed testimonies based on visions or dreams and took other actions to end the trials. By the new year most of the accused were released, and the trials ended.

Witches in Modern Times

Witches were seldom tried and executed after the 1800s, but people who claimed to be witches still existed. Witches met in secrecy until the 1950s when writer and practicing witch Gerald Gardner published several books about Wicca, including *Witchcraft Today* and *The Meaning of Witchcraft*. More people began to take an interest in Wicca and most countries abolished their antiwitchcraft laws. Although Wicca is one of the world's fastest-growing religions, with thousands of members, many Wiccans continue to be persecuted and misunderstood.

Helen Duncan

Helen Duncan was a Scottish **medium** who lived in Britain during World War II. She frequently held **séances** during which, it was said, she was able to make the spirits of the dead appear and even talk with their family members. Often, the spirits were soldiers who had died in battle. In 1944, at a séance attended by several people, she caused a sailor from the HMS *Barham* to appear. This was a problem because the fact that the ship had been sunk by the Germans was a military secret that had not yet been released to the public. A short time later a plain-clothes policeman attended one of Duncan's séances and arrested her.

She was convicted under an old 1735 witchcraft law and served nine months in prison. Many people, including Prime Minister Winston Churchill, believed that she was unfairly convicted because the authorities thought that she really

Helen Duncan's granddaughter, Mary Martin (pictured, holding a photo of Duncan), feels her grandmother was wrongly convicted of witchcraft in 1944. She is seeking a pardon for Duncan in order to clear her grandmother's name.

Do No Harm

Many people believe that witches cast evil spells. However, one of the most important creeds in the Wiccan religion is the idea that witches should not cause harm. Many Wiccans believe that any harm they cause will come back to them tripled.

could see the future and would leak top secret military information. Churchill repealed the ancient witchcraft law in 1951.

As of 2007, Duncan's granddaughter, 72-year-old Mary Martin, has been working to get the British government to **pardon** her grandmother. She still has vivid memories of being teased as a child when Duncan was arrested. "The memories are still fresh. It was so unfair. She was totally innocent. It was ludicrous she was ever taken to court,"[8] says Martin.

Zsuzsanna Budapest

Like Helen Duncan, Zsuzsanna Budapest was also arrested for practicing her craft. She has dedicated her life to goddess spirituality and has been a practicing witch for many years. In 1975 she was arrested and convicted for reading tarot cards in Los Angeles. At that time, telling the future for other people was against the law. She was fined $300.

Reading tarot cards, which some people believe can be used to predict the future, is viewed as a form of witchcraft by many people.

As required, Budapest stopped reading tarot for other people. Instead, she started to teach classes on tarot and witchcraft. Since the law was about reading tarot cards for other people and not about teaching people how to do it themselves, she could not be arrested again. The law against predicting people's futures was repealed in 1981.

Teenage Witch

Adult witches are not the only ones who have been punished for practicing witchcraft. In October 1998 high school sophomore Jennifer Rassan broke down in hysterics when she thought that fellow student Jamie Schoonover, a practicing witch, had put a hex on her. When Jennifer told the school's administrators, Jamie was suspended from school because the administrators considered the hex to be a verbal threat.

The girls, their parents, and the administrators met that afternoon. Jamie claimed that she did not cast a spell on Jennifer and that her Wiccan beliefs would prevent her from causing harm to another person. Although the suspension was revoked, Jamie asked to be transferred to another school. According to her mother, the incident was one of several resulting from "ignorance about witchcraft."[9] Jamie had been taunted by other students for her Wiccan beliefs. "She dresses differently and listens to different kinds of music,"[10] said her mother. Even though no spell was cast, after the meeting Jennifer claimed to still be frightened of Jamie.

Prejudice against witches still exists today. Here, a young follower of Wicca leaves court after suing her high school for the right to wear a pentagram, the Wicca symbol, which had previously been banned.

Selling the Craft

Some modern witches perform spells, tell fortunes, and dispense potions for money. Critics say that these people cannot really do magic and are just taking advantage of people in need.

Harassed for Beliefs

Unlike Jamie, Jean Webb did not practice her Wiccan beliefs openly. She and her two teenagers hid their Wiccan faith when they moved to the small town of Republic, Missouri, in 1995. Webb was afraid that even though the people seemed nice, they might not understand her Wiccan beliefs.

Webb got a job writing for the local newspaper and things were fine until the spring of 1998 when she wrote an editorial protesting the use of the Christian fish symbol on the town seal. Webb was fired soon after, and people began to harass her and her family. She frequently received threatening phone calls, and the checker at the grocery store refused to serve her. In addition, her daughter received so much abuse from classmates that Webb began to homeschool her.

Webb eventually moved to Springfield, Missouri, but she continued to fight for her beliefs in

Republic. With the help of the American Civil Liberties Union (ACLU), Webb sued the city to have the symbol removed. She felt that fighting the city was the right thing to do because the symbol "is not only a violation of the constitutional separation of church and state but also a signal that Republic is a town where only Christians are welcome."[11] In the end, the judge agreed with Webb and the ACLU and ruled that the symbol had to be removed from the town seal.

Witch School

Many people in the small town of Hoopeston, Illinois, were upset when they heard that there would soon be a witch school right in the middle of their town. The school, which is devoted to teaching people about Wicca, provides most of its classes online and has over 100,000 students from all over the world. Students can enroll in Internet courses on a wide range of subjects including spell casting,

The Witch School in Hoopeston, Illinois, was established to educate people who want to learn about Wicca. Here, students are participating in a Wiccan lunar ritual.

Students at the Witch School can learn about all subjects having to do with the practice of witchcraft.

herbalism, tarot reading, and the histories of pagan cultures. In the summer of 2003 director Ed Hubbard decided the school should exist in the real world as well as on the Internet.

Hubbard's plan to open his school in Hoopeston was met with a great deal of opposition from the mostly Christian town. Some of the residents were afraid of the witches and of the spells they might cast. A few people even blamed a period of bad weather on the school, saying that the town had been cursed. Over 400 residents signed petitions to stop the school from opening. Several pastors of local churches held prayer meetings with the same goal. Hubbard received hundreds of calls and e-mails telling him that his school was not wanted in Hoopeston. At a town counsel meeting on the opening of the school, Hubbard said, "What I'm hearing today is that because I'm a Wiccan, I am not welcome, regardless of the fact that I'm American."[12]

Hubbard was frightened by the people's response and he nearly gave up. But he also received support from people who felt he had a right to build his school wherever he wished. Hubbard decided to go forward, and the school opened on September 1, 2003. Today the school holds daily classes and welcomes visitors. Two other pagan-owned businesses have opened in Hoopeston as well. According to the Witch School Web site, "We have more than a hundred visitors on any given weekend. We are developing our own press including the Daily Spell and Magick TV, our own shops, and our own way of doing things. . . . We are steadily integrating ourselves with this small community."[13]

The Witch Next Door

While some Wiccans practice their craft publicly, many others continue to practice in secret because they feel they will be misunderstood. This means that people encounter witches every day without knowing it. Mothers, teachers, bakers, bankers—anyone might be Wiccan. Other Wiccans such as Zsuzsanna Budapest and Ed Hubbard do not hide their beliefs. Instead, they work to educate people about Wicca so Wiccans can practice their craft without fear.

Notes

Chapter 1: Witches Yesterday and Today

1. Exodus 22:18 (New International Version).
2. Zsuzsanna Budapest, Gratefulness.org. www.gratefulness.org/box/item.cfm?qbox_id=189.

Chapter 2: The Witches' Wrath

3. Quoted in Ronald Seth. *Children Against Witches*, New York: Taplinger, 1969, p. 53.
4. Quoted in *The Pendle Witches*. www.pendlewitches.co.uk/content.php?page=alizon.
5. Quoted in Frank Luttmer, *Chelmsford Witches*. http://history.hanover.edu/courses/excerpts/26chelm.html.

Chapter 3: Witch Hunts

6. Quoted in Alan C. Kors and Edward Peters, *Witchcraft in Europe, 1100–1700: A Documentary History*. University of Pennsylvania Press, 1972.
7. Quoted in Essex County Archives, *Salem: Witchcraft*, vol. 1, p. 10. http://etext.lib.virginia.edu/etcbin/toccer-new2?id=BoySal2.sgm&images=images/moeng&data=/texts/english/modeng/oldsalem&tag=public&part=272&divi sion=div2.

Chapter 4: Witches in Modern Times

8. Quoted in Reuters, "Family Seeks Pardon for Last Convicted Witch," January 15, 2007. www.msnbc.msn.com/id/16635110/?GT1=8921.
9. Quoted in Paul W. Valentine, *Washington Post*, "Student Suspended over 'Hex'", October 22, 1998.
10. Quoted in Paul W. Valentine, "Student Suspended over 'Hex'".
11. Quoted in John Rogers, Associated Press, "Witch Fights Christian Town" October 18, 1998.
12. Quoted in Bethany Caron and Mary Lou Brackman "Vocal Opposition Pushes Wiccan School Out of Hoopeston" *The Chronicle*, July 2, 2003 available online at http://www.thehoopestonchronicle.com/articles/2003/07/02/news/news01.txt.
13. Witch School Campus http://www.witchschool.com/campus.asp.

Glossary

coven: A gathering of witches, usually thirteen in number.

familiar: A spirit in the form of an animal belonging to a witch.

incantation: The chanting of magic words.

medium: A person who claims to be able to communicate with the spirits of the dead.

midwife: A woman skilled in assisting a woman in childbirth.

pagan: Ancient religions that worship many gods.

pardon: Forgiveness granted from an official source for committing a crime.

persecute: To systematically treat a person or group cruelly or unfairly because of their race or beliefs.

Puritans: A group of English Protestants who believed in strict religious discipline.

rheumatism: A painful condition affecting the joints and muscles.

ritual: A set of actions performed as part of a ceremony.

séance: A meeting during which people try to make contact with the spirits of the dead.

sorcery: Supernatural power gained from evil spirits.

strappado: A form of torture in which somebody is lifted off the ground by a rope around the wrists, which have been tied behind his or her back. The person is then dropped and jerked to a stop just before reaching the ground.

superstitious: Belief that is based on fear of the supernatural or luck rather than on human reason or scientific knowledge.

thumbscrews: An instrument of torture that was used to crush people's thumbs and fingers.

For Further Exploration

Books

David Bennett, *The Kingfisher Treasury of Witch and Wizard Stories*. Boston, MA: Kingfisher, 2004. An illustrated collection of fifteen stories about witches and wizards.

Tracey Boraas, *The Salem Witch Trials (Let Freedom Ring)*. Mankato, MN: Capstone Press: 2006. This book details the events of the Salem witch trials. Includes glossary and timeline.

Douglas Hill, *Eyewitness: Witches & Magic Makers*. New York: DK Publishing, 2000. This colorful book includes information on witches in other cultures, witches in fiction, witch hunts, and magical items.

Adam McKeown, *The Young Reader's Shakespeare: Macbeth*, New York: Sterling Publishing, 2006. This illustrated, kid-friendly retelling of Macbeth incorporates many of the original passages and includes an informative introduction and questions section.

Gwinevere Rain, *Spellcraft for Teens: A Magickal Guide to Writing & Casting Spells*. St Paul, MN: Llewellyn Publications, 2002. Written by a practicing teenage witch, this guide gives the aspiring witch a wealth of information about the Wiccan religion.

Jane Yolen, *The Salem Witch Trials: An Unsolved Mystery from History*. New York: Simon and Schuster Books for Young Readers, 2004. This well-illustrated book presents the trials in a fun mystery format. With informative sidebars and peeks into the investigator's notebook, this book invites readers to form their own conclusions about the trials.

Web Sites

The Bell Witch (www.bellwitch.org./). Site devoted to all aspects of the Bell witch legend.

Llewellyn Teens and Tweens: Wicca (www.llewellyn.com/teen/wicca. php). Website includes FAQs about Wicca, advice, and horoscopes for young Wiccans.

Salem Witchcraft Hysteria (http://72.14.253.104/search?q=cache:7VQWP1ryl6oJ:www.nationalgeographic.com/salem/+witch+hunt+interactive&hl=en&gl=us&ct=clnk&cd=1). *National Geographic*'s simulation makes you an accused witch in Salem.

Salem Witch Trials (http://school.discovery.com/schooladventures/salemwitchtrials/). Information on the Salem witch trials from the Discovery School. Includes a short movie.

Index

Picture Credits

About the Author

Rachel Lynette is not a witch, but some of her friends are. She has written over a dozen other books for children as well as many articles on children and family life. She also teaches science to children of all ages. Rachel lives in the Seattle area in the Songaia Cohousing Community with her two children, David and Lucy, a cat named Cosette, and two playful rats. When she isn't teaching or writing she enjoys spending time with her family and friends, traveling, reading, drawing, crocheting, and inline skating.